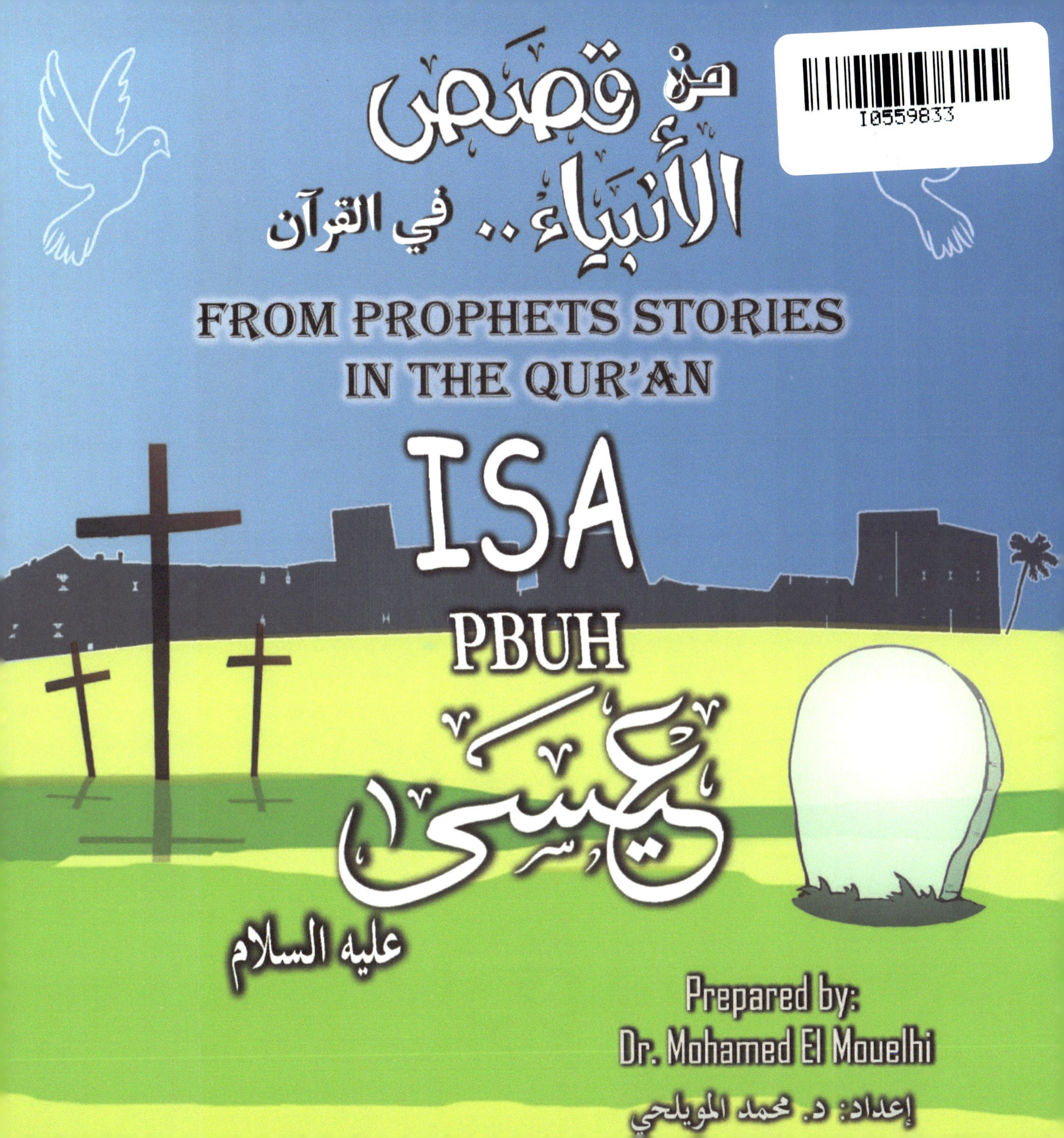

من قصص الأنبياء .. في القرآن

FROM PROPHETS STORIES IN THE QUR'AN

ISA
PBUH

عِيسَى
عليه السلام

Prepared by:
Dr. Mohamed El Mouelhi

إعداد: د. محمد المويلحي

To My Grandchildren, My Inspiration.
-Giddo M.

ISBN 978-1-959536-07-9
First edition 2024

Published by Honey Elm Books LLC
www.HoneyElmBooks.com

ISA *PBUH*

عيسى عليه السلام

Editing: Noha Elmouelhi

Artistic Preparation: Hossam El Mouelhi - Donia Farouk

تحرير: نهى المويلحي

الإعداد الفني: حسام المويلحي- دنيا فاروق

**Allah chose some individuals
to be preferred over all mankind.
Among them were the Prophets and their
ancestry starting with Adam, then Nuh, and Ibrahim.
Al-Imran were from Ibrahim's dynasty.
mran's wife did not have children and prayed to Allah to
bless her with a child to service the house of Allah .**

إختار الله بعض البشر وفضلهم بين الناس، ومن بينهم سلالة الأنبياء بدءًا
من آدم، ثم نوح، ثم إبراهيم. وآل عمران هم من سلالة
إبراهيم عليه السلام. ولم يكن لزوجة عمران أولادًا
فدعت الله أن يرزقها بطفل ليقوم بخدمة بيت الله.

Allah answered her prayers
and she was gifted with a baby girl.
She called her Maryam
meaning "Servant of Lord",
and prayed to Allah to protect her and her progeny
from Satan.
She dedicated her to serving Allah and his religion.

فاستجاب لها الله ووضعت بنتًا وسمتها مريم –أى خادمة الرب – ودعت الله أن يحفظها وذريتها من الشيطان الرجيم. ووهبت إبنتها مريم للعبادة وخدمة الدين.

` "... and I have named her Maryam,
and I seek refuge with You for her
and for her offspring from Satan, the rejected." '
(Al-Imran: 36)

بِسْمِ اللَّهِ الرَّحْمَنِ الرَّحِيمِ

... وَإِنِّي سَمَّيْتُهَا مَرْيَمَ وَإِنِّي أُعِيذُهَا بِكَ
وَذُرِّيَّتَهَا مِنَ الشَّيْطَانِ الرَّجِيمِ ﴿٣٦﴾

Allah blessed Maryam
and made her life easy and provided her
with an abundance of blessings.
She spent her days worshiping Allah.
Because of her devotion to her religion, Allah chose her to
be the miraculous mother of Prophet Isa with no father.
This miracle was divine proof of Allah's ability to command
things to be and they are.

بارك الله فى مريم ويسر لها حياتها ورزقها رزقًا كثيرًا من الطيبات، وكانت مريم
كثيرة العبادة والتفكر فى الله سبحانه وتعالى لذلك إختارها الله لتحمل
معجزته المسيح عيسى عليه السلام من غير أب، وكانت هذه المعجزة
دليلا على قدرة الله على خلق ما يشاء وأنه إذا أراد شيئا
فيقول له كن فيكون.

' ... He said: "So for Allah creates
what He wills.
When He has decreed something,
He says to it only: Be! - and it is"
(Al-Imran: 47)

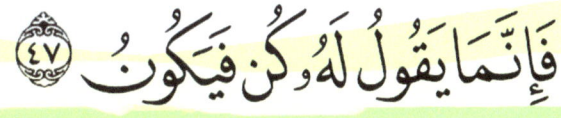

Maryam returned
with her new baby to her people
who wondered how she had a baby
while a virgin?
She told her people that Isa was a miracle from Allah
and that they can ask him if they did not believe her.
Her people did not believe her; how could a newborn
baby speak? Right then, Isa spoke and told them he was Allah's
Prophet and that he was sent to deliver Allah's Message.
Allah gave Isa wisdom and sent him a divine revelation
- the Bible (Injil).

وبعد أن وضعت مريم طفلها ذهبت به الى قومها، فتعجبوا من كيفية إنجاب
طفل لمريم العذراء؟ فأخبرتهم مريم أنه معجزة من الله ويمكنهم
سؤاله، فقالوا هذا مستحيل أن يستطيع طفل رضيع الكلام في هذا
السن الصغير، وعندها أخبرهم عيسى أنه عبد الله وأنه رسوله
لتبليغ قومه رسالة السماء. وقد علمه الله الحكمة
وأنزل عليه الكتاب السماوي وهو الإنجيل.

' He said: "Verily! I am a slave of Allah,
He has given me the Scripture and made
me a Prophet;" '
(Maryam: 30)

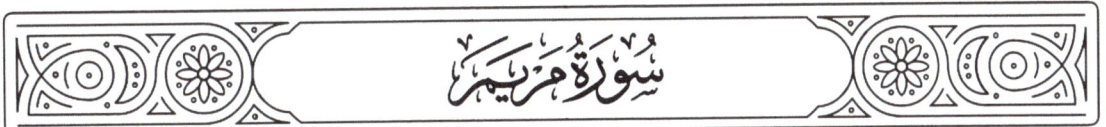

بِسْمِ اللهِ الرَّحْمَنِ الرَّحِيمِ

قَالَ إِنِّي عَبْدُ اللهِ ءَاتَنِيَ ٱلْكِتَبَ وَجَعَلَنِي نَبِيًّا ۝

Allah had given Isa
some miracles as evidence
for his prophethood.
By Allah's Will, he was able to make a bird statue
to fly by breathing in it, cure blind people
and patients with leprosy, and revive the dead
by Allah's Permission. All these miracles were gifted
to him by Allah to enforce his message to
the Children of Israel that came after Musa.

وأعطى الله عيسى عليه السلام بعض المعجزات كي تكون دليلا على كونه
رسولًا من عند الله، فقد أتاه الله القدرة على عمل تمثال يشبه الطير ثم ينفخ
فيه فيصبح طيرًا يطير، وأيضًا قدرته على شفاء المرضى بالعمى
والجزام، كما أنعم الله عليه بمعجزة إحياء الموتى كل ذلك
بإذن الله تعالى. وأعطى الله لعيسى كل هذه المعجزات لإقناع
قوم بني إسرائيل الذين جاؤا بعد موسى
عليه السلام بصدق رسالته .

` " ... I design for you out of clay,

a figure like that of a bird, and breathe into it,

and it becomes a bird by Allah's Permission; and I heal

who was born blind, and the leper, and I bring the dead

to life by Allah's Permission.... " '

(Al-Imran: 49)

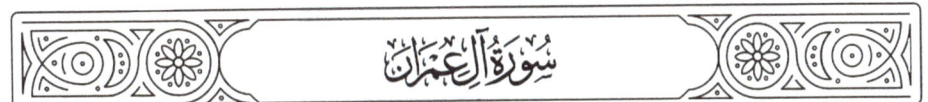

بِسْمِ اللَّهِ الرَّحْمَٰنِ الرَّحِيمِ

... أَنِّي أَخْلُقُ لَكُم مِّنَ ٱلطِّينِ كَهَيْئَةِ ٱلطَّيْرِ فَأَنفُخُ

فِيهِ فَيَكُونُ طَيْرًا بِإِذْنِ ٱللَّهِ وَأُبْرِئُ ٱلْأَكْمَهَ وَٱلْأَبْرَصَ

وَأُحْيِ ٱلْمَوْتَىٰ بِإِذْنِ ٱللَّهِ ... ﴿٤٩﴾

When the Children of Israel
deserted their religion,
Allah sent Isa to them to call them back
to the right way of worshiping Allah.
Some of his people believed him;
they were called 'Apostles'.

وقد أرسل الله عيسى عليه السلام الى بنى إسرائيل عندما إبتعدوا عن تعاليم دينهم وذلك لدعوتهم لعبادة الله كما يجب، فآمن له البعض منهم وهم الحواريون.

The apostles, those who believed in Isa's message, asked Isa to pray to Allah to provide them with a meal from heaven to strengthen their faith and remove any doubt from their heart. Isa prayed to Allah to send to them a meal from heaven to be a feast for them and proof for his prophethood.

وأراد الذين آمنوا برسالته– وهم الحواريون – أن تطمئن قلوبهم ويزداد إيمانهم، فسألوا عيسى أن يطلب من الله أن ينزل عليهم مائدة من السماء يأكلوا مما عليها ويزيلوا أى شك فى صدورهم. فدعا عيسى ربه أن يمُنّ عليهم ويرسل لهم وجبة يأكلوا منها تكون عيدًا لهم ودليلًا قويًا على نبوته.

12

`(Remember) when the apostles
said: "O Isa, son of Maryam! Can your Lord
send down to us a table spread (with food)
from heaven?" Isa said: "Fear Allah, if you are indeed
believers." ʻ
(Al-Maeda: 112)

إِذْ قَالَ الْحَوَارِيُّونَ يَعِيسَى ابْنَ مَرْيَمَ هَلْ يَسْتَطِيعُ رَبُّكَ
أَن يُنَزِّلَ عَلَيْنَا مَآئِدَةً مِّنَ السَّمَآءِ قَالَ اتَّقُوا اللَّهَ إِن كُنتُم
مُّؤْمِنِينَ ﴿١١٢﴾

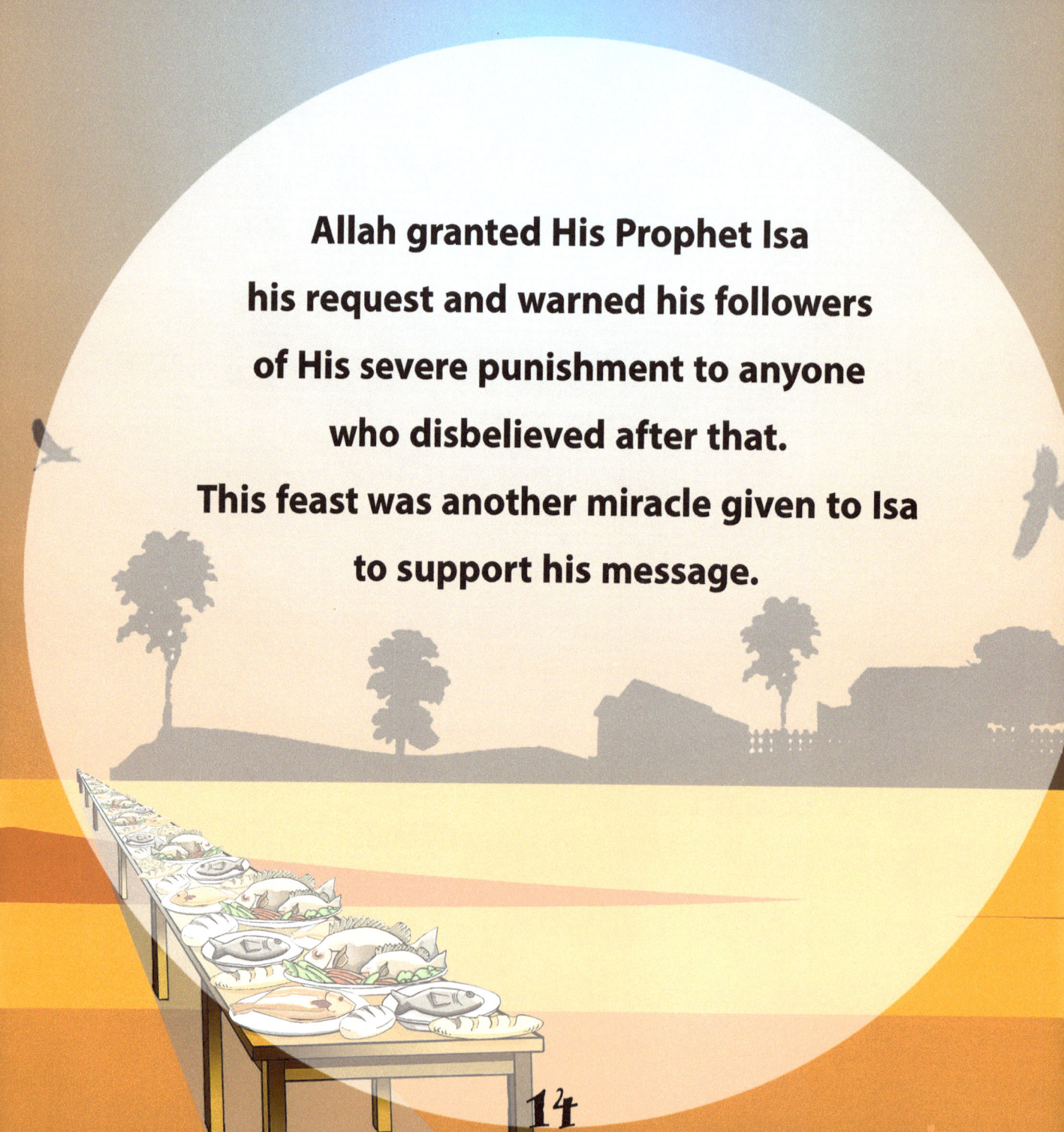

Allah granted His Prophet Isa
his request and warned his followers
of His severe punishment to anyone
who disbelieved after that.
This feast was another miracle given to Isa
to support his message.

14

فأستجاب الله لطلب عيسى وأخبره أن من يكفر بعد ذلك سيكون له عذابًا شديدًا، وهذه معجزة أخرى أختص الله بها نبيه عيسى عليه السلام تأكيدًا لصدق رسالته.

Isa was one of the messengers
to the Children of Israel.
He told them that there will be another
messenger coming after him
and that this messenger's name means the most praising
person to God Almighty.

عيسى عليه السلام
هو أحد أنبياء بني إسرائيل وقد أخبرهم أنه سيأتى
من بعده رسول من الله وأشار الى إسمه، والذى يعنى
أنه أحمد الناس لله سبحانه وتعالى.

'And (remember)

when Isa, son of Maryam,

said: "O Children of Israel! I am the Messenger

of Allah unto you confirming the Taurah which

came before me, and giving glad tidings of a

Messenger to come after me, whose name

shall be Ahmed ....." '

(Al-Saff: 6)

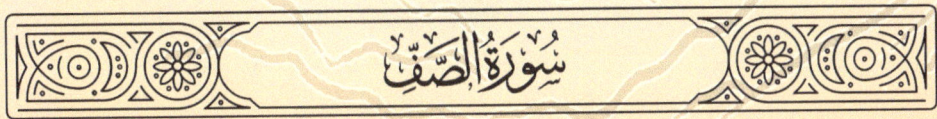

بِسْمِ اللَّهِ الرَّحْمَٰنِ الرَّحِيمِ

وَإِذْ قَالَ عِيسَى ابْنُ مَرْيَمَ يَٰبَنِي إِسْرَٰٓءِيلَ إِنِّي رَسُولُ اللَّهِ إِلَيْكُم مُّصَدِّقًا لِّمَا

بَيْنَ يَدَيَّ مِنَ التَّوْرَىٰةِ وَمُبَشِّرًا بِرَسُولٍ يَأْتِي مِنۢ بَعْدِي اسْمُهُۥٓ أَحْمَدُ ..... ﴿٦﴾

Despite all the miracles
bestowed by Allah on His Prophet Isa,
a group of people disbelieved him
and his message.
They plotted to crucify and kill him.
Would Allah allow them to do that?

وعلى الرغم من كل المعجزات التى أختص الله بها نبيه عيسى عليه السلام
فقد كذّب بعض القوم به وبرسالته، وتآمروا عليه
لصلبه وقتله.
فهل سيسمح الله لهم بذلك؟

Of course not.

Almighty Allah did not allow them to hurt

His Prophet.

Before they could kill him,

Allah raised Isa to heaven to save him from

his enemies and the enemies of the religion of Allah.

بالطبع لا، فإن الله سبحانه وتعالى لم يدعهم يؤذوا نبيه
ويعذبوه، بل رفعه الله إليه لينجيه من أيدى أعدائه وأعداء الدين.

'And because of their saying,
"We killed Isa, son of Maryam,
the Messenger of Allah," - but they killed him not,
nor crucified him,
but it seemed like this to them,
and those who differ therein are full of doubts.
They have no knowledge; they follow nothing
but conjecture.
For surely; they killed him not (157)
But Allah raised him up unto Himself.
And Allah is Ever All-Powerful, All-Wise.' (158)
(Al-Nisaa: 157-158)

20

بِسْمِ اللَّهِ الرَّحْمَٰنِ الرَّحِيمِ

وَقَوْلِهِمْ إِنَّا قَتَلْنَا ٱلْمَسِيحَ عِيسَى ٱبْنَ مَرْيَمَ رَسُولَ ٱللَّهِ وَمَا قَتَلُوهُ وَمَا صَلَبُوهُ وَلَٰكِن شُبِّهَ لَهُمْ ۚ وَإِنَّ ٱلَّذِينَ ٱخْتَلَفُوا۟ فِيهِ لَفِى شَكٍّ مِّنْهُ ۚ مَا لَهُم بِهِۦ مِنْ عِلْمٍ إِلَّا ٱتِّبَاعَ ٱلظَّنِّ ۚ وَمَا قَتَلُوهُ يَقِينًۢا ﴿١٥٧﴾ بَل رَّفَعَهُ ٱللَّهُ إِلَيْهِ ۚ وَكَانَ ٱللَّهُ عَزِيزًا حَكِيمًا ﴿١٥٨﴾

After some time,

people started to wonder about Isa

and his miraculous birth.

Allah mentions in the Qur'an the similarity

between Isa and Adam.

Both of them were created by the will of Allah: Be and they

Were. Adam was created without a mother or a father, and Is

was created with a mother but no father.

Glory be to God, the Creator of everything.

تساءل الناس عن كيفية خلق المسيح عيسى وأثاروا الشكوك

حول هذه المعجزة، فأوضح الله لهم التشابه فى خلق

كل من آدم وعيسى، فكلاهما قال الله له كن فكان، وقد خلق الله

آدم من غير أم ولا أب، أما عيسى فقد خلقه الله من أم

ولكن بلا أب.

سبحان الله الخالق لكل شىء.

`Verily, the likeness of Isa before Allah

is the likeness of Adam.

He created him from dust, then (He) said to him: "Be!"

– and he was.'

(Al-Imran:59)

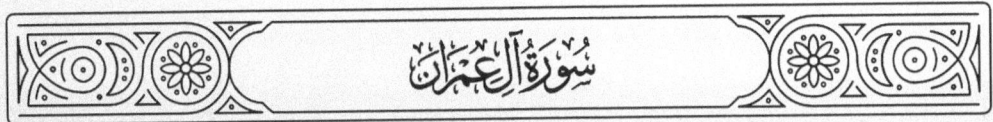

بِسْمِ اللّٰهِ الرَّحْمٰنِ الرَّحِيمِ

إِنَّ مَثَلَ عِيسَىٰ عِندَ ٱللَّهِ كَمَثَلِ ءَادَمَ خَلَقَهُۥ مِن تُرَابٍ ثُمَّ قَالَ لَهُۥ كُن فَيَكُونُ ۝

ALLAH BESTOWED MANY MIRACLES ON HIS PROPHET ISA.

Some of which are:

- Creating him from a mother with no father.

- Speaking as a baby to prove his mother's virginity and innocence.

- Crafting bird statue that flew by Allah's Command.

- Curing blindness and leprosy by Allah's Will.

- Revival of the dead by Allah's Permission.

- The table feast descent from heaven.

- Being saved from crucification and being raised to heaven.

Glory be to God, if He wants something, He says to it, be, and it is.

أنعم الله على المسيح عيسى بمعجزات عديدة
منها :

– خلقه الله من أم بلا أب .

– النطق ببراءة أمه وهو طفل فى مهده .

– صناعته للطيور التى تطير بإذن الله .

– شفاء الأعمى ومريض الجزام بإذن الله .

– إحياء الموتى بإذن الله وأمره .

– إنزال المائدة من السماء .

– نجاته من عذاب بنى إسرائيل ورفعه إلى السماء قبل أن
يصلبوه ويقتلوه فعلا .

سبحان اللّه إذا أراد شيئًا يقول له كن فيكون .

We learn many lessons
from the story of Isa PBUH.
Here are a few:
- The strong belief in Allah's Decree and dedication
to His Worship.
- All miracles are granted by Allah to support
His Prophets to deliver His Message.
- To reflect on the divine miracles as proof of Allah's Power.
- Allah is our Guide and Protector.

قصة عيسى عليه السلام تحتوى على نقاط تعليمية هامة عديدة
ومنها:
– الإيمان القوى بقدر الله، والتفانى الكامل فى عبادته.
– يمُنُ الله على أنبيائه ورسله بالمعجزات لمساندتهم فى تبليغ رسالته.
– التفكر فى المعجزات الإلهية الدالة على قدرة الخالق.
– الله هو الهادى والحافظ.

ISA PBUH
عيسى عليه السلام

MUHAMMAD PBUH
محمد عليه الصلاة والسلام

ZAKARIYA PBUH
زكريا عليه السلام

ILYAS PBUH
إلياس عليه السلام

ALYASA PBUH
اليسع عليه السلام

YAHYA PBUH
يحيى عليه السلام

SULAIMAN PBUH
سليمان عليه السلام

MUSA PBUH
موسى عليه السلام

HAROON PBUH
هارون عليه السلام

YUSUF PBUH
يوسف عليه السلام

YUNUS PBUH
يونس عليه السلام

DAWOOD PBUH
داود عليه السلام

YAQUB PBUH
يعقوب عليه السلام

ISMAIL PBUH
إسماعيل عليه السلام

SHUAIB PBUH
شعيب عليه السلام

ISHAQ PBUH
إسحاق عليه السلام

DHUL KIFL PBUH
ذو الكفل عليه السلام

AYYUB PBUH
أيوب عليه السلام

IBRAHIM PBUH
إبراهيم عليه السلام

HUD PBUH
هود عليه السلام

LUT PBUH
لوط عليه السلام

NUH PBUH
نوح عليه السلام

SALIH PBUH
صالح عليه السلام

IDRIS PBUH
إدريس عليه السلام

ADAM PBUH
آدم عليه السلام

Isa PBUH,
Allah blessed him
with many miracles
including his birth.

عيسى عليه السلام
خصه الله بمعجزات كثيرة
ومنها مولده

27

Watch a special reading of Isa PBUH by the author!

Scan this QR code to access the video.